Facts About the Centipede

By Lisa Strattin

© 2019 Lisa Strattin

FREE BOOK

FREE FOR ALL SUBSCRIBERS

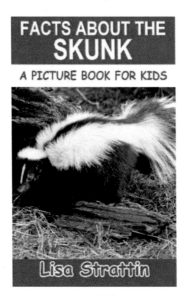

LisaStrattin.com/Subscribe-Here

BOX SET

- **FACTS ABOUT THE POISON DART FROGS**
- **FACTS ABOUT THE THREE TOED SLOTH**
- **FACTS ABOUT THE RED PANDA**
- **FACTS ABOUT THE SEAHORSE**
- **FACTS ABOUT THE PLATYPUS**
- **FACTS ABOUT THE REINDEER**
- **FACTS ABOUT THE PANTHER**
- **FACTS ABOUT THE SIBERIAN HUSKY**

LisaStrattin.com/BookBundle

Facts for Kids Picture Books by Lisa Strattin

Little Blue Penguin, Vol 92

Chipmunk, Vol 5

Frilled Lizard, Vol 39

Blue and Gold Macaw, Vol 13

Poison Dart Frogs, Vol 50

Blue Tarantula, Vol 115

African Elephants, Vol 8

Amur Leopard, Vol 89

Sabre Tooth Tiger, Vol 167

Baboon, Vol 174

Sign Up for New Release Emails Here

LisaStrattin.com/subscribe-here

COVER IMAGE

https://www.flickr.com/photos/chodhound/5170595620/

ADDITIONAL IMAGES

https://www.flickr.com/photos/prkos/1000187444/

https://www.flickr.com/photos/nh53/8357589857/

https://www.flickr.com/photos/schizoform/42145142/

https://www.flickr.com/photos/36319440@N05/5647341899/

https://www.flickr.com/photos/mattx27/7616297484/

https://www.flickr.com/photos/14583963@N00/7272271450/

https://www.flickr.com/photos/adavey/5051703601/

https://www.flickr.com/photos/14583963@N00/7855669800/

https://www.flickr.com/photos/elchode/36387658190/

https://www.flickr.com/photos/mifaleelphoto/16068394072

Contents

INTRODUCTION

Even though the name of the Centipede implies that they have 100 legs, this is not true. They normally have between 15 to 30 pairs of legs, not 50.

Researchers believe that there are 8,000 different species of centipede in the world, but only 3,000 have been studied.

3,000 different ones!

That's a lot of different Centipedes!

CHARACTERISTICS

Many of the Centipede species don't even have eyes!

They locate their prey by using their antennae, sensing vibrations as a small insect goes by, the Centipede catches them.

However, some do have eyes, and with or without eyes, they are ferocious predators, as they hunt for prey.

APPEARANCE

Every species of Centipede has an odd number of pairs of legs, this means that none of them really has 50 pairs – which would mean 100 legs – since 50 is an even number.

They have a flat or round head, depending on the species, two antennae, and long, slender jaws. Their first pair of legs stretch out forward instead of toward the side and have sharp claws that can release venom to paralyze their prey.

REPRODUCTION

The female Centipede lays around 60 eggs at a time. This is called a "clutch." She will usually bury them in dirt to protect them from predators. The female guards them until they hatch. Once they hatch, some mothers continue to guard them until they are ready to take off on their own.Some species of Centipede babies actually kill their mother!

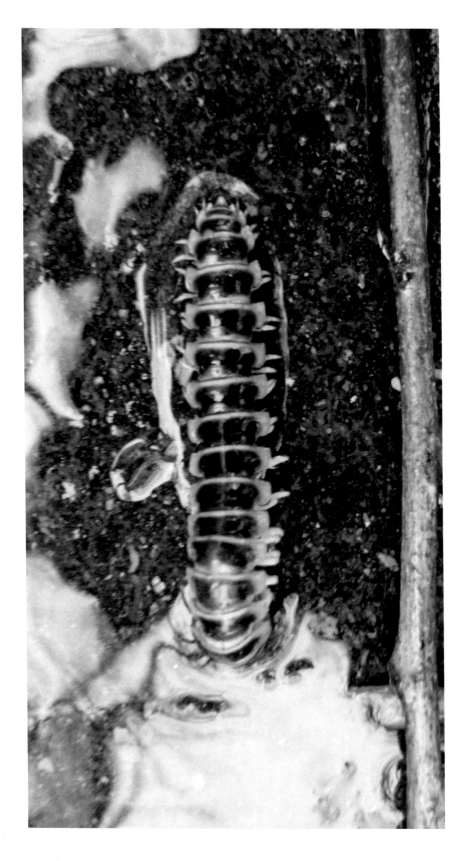

LIFE SPAN

If the Centipede is able to avoid predators, they have been observed to live up to 6 years!

SIZE

Since there are so many different Centipede species, it is understandable that they can be very small and surprisingly large.

The smallest Centipede is only about 1/10th of an inch in length, while the largest one (that we know about), the Amazonian Giant Centipede, can grow to be 12 inches long!

HABITAT

Centipedes seem to be able to live all over the World in wet regions. They like to live in damp areas – under leaves, rocks, and logs, in rotting wood, or even in the ground. They have even been found in the Arctic Circle!

They don't care much for deserts though, so you won't see a lot of them in hot, dry areas.

DIET

The Centipede is a dominant predator in the world of insects.

They eat spiders, earthworms, and other insects.

The largest known Centipede, the Amazonian Giant Centipede, eats frogs, lizards, mice, birds and bats. They even catch bats and birds as they are flying by!

Did you know that any Centipede was big and strong enough to eat a mouse or a bat?

ENEMIES

The Centipede has to watch out for many predators in the World. After all, most of the Centipedes are pretty small.

Frogs, Toads, birds and other small mammals, like mice, will hunt and eat many species of Centipedes.

SUITABILITY AS PETS

You could probably have a Centipede as a pet, if you want to. Although, the Amazonian Giant Centipede might not be a good choice.

Centipedes do bite, and it will hurt if one bites you.

But many people like to have different insects for pets, just check with your parents before you decide to keep one!

COLOR ME

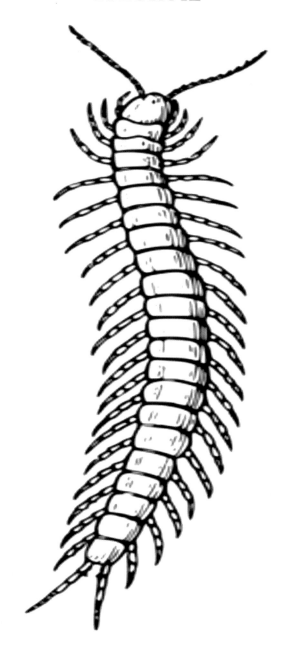

29

COLOR ME

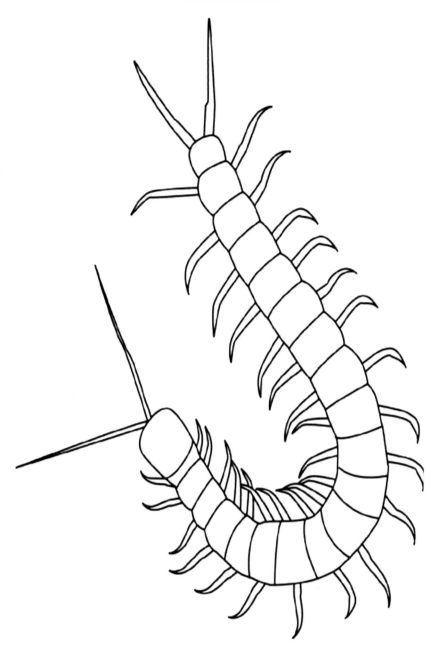

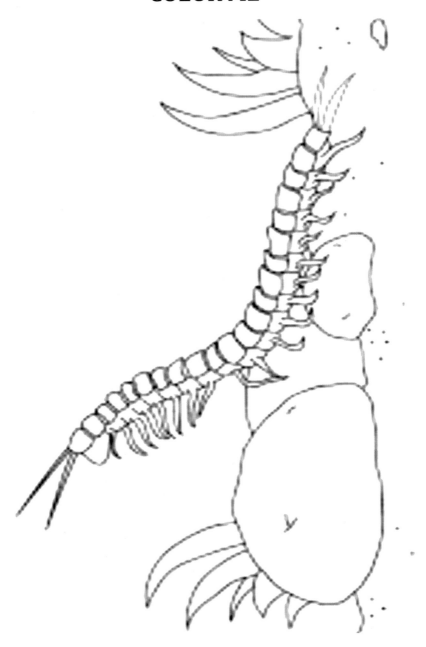

COLOR ME

COLOR ME

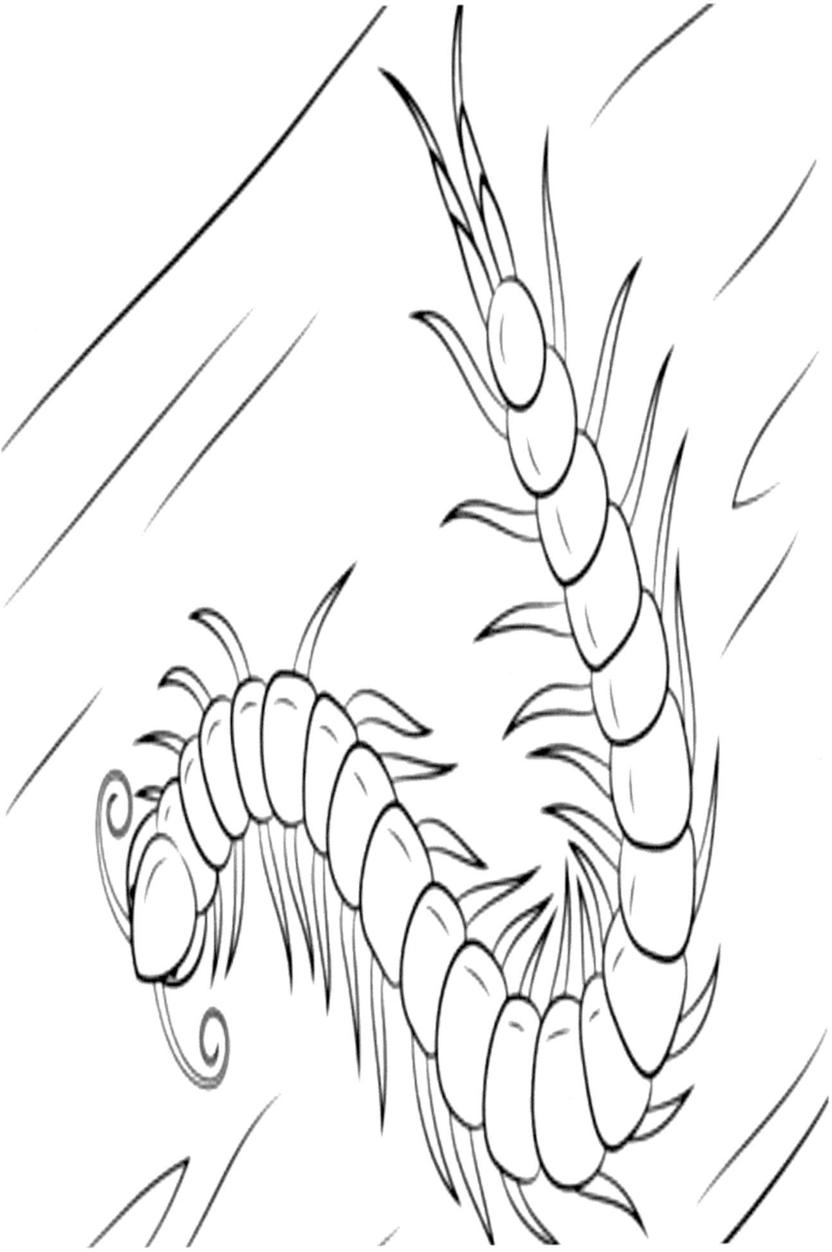

COLOR ME

COLOR ME

COLOR ME

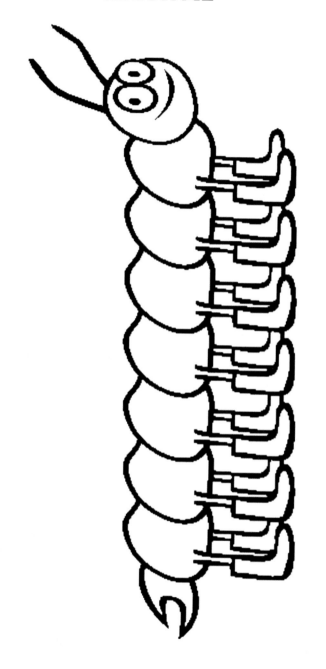

COLOR ME

Please leave me a review here:

LisaStrattin.com/Review-Vol-355

For more Kindle Downloads Visit Lisa Strattin Author Page on Amazon Author Central

amazon.com/author/lisastrattin

To see upcoming titles, visit my website at LisaStrattin.com– most books available on Kindle!

LisaStrattin.com

FREE BOOK

FOR ALL SUBSCRIBERS – SIGN UP NOW

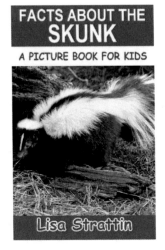

LisaStrattin.com/Subscribe-Here

LisaStrattin.com/Facebook

LisaStrattin.com/Youtube

Made in the USA
Columbia, SC
14 January 2022

54257273R00024